Cooking in the Nude

RED HOT LOVERS

Edited by Cameron Brown and Katherine A. Neale
Designed by Carolyn Weary Brandt

First published in 1987 by Wellton Books.
Revised, expanded edition copyright © 1995 by Debbie and Stephen Cornwell.
All rights reserved.

Library of Congress Catalog Card Number 95-81868
ISBN 0-943231-98-1

Printed in the United States of America
Published by Howell Press, Inc., 1713-2D Allied Lane,
Charlottesville, Virginia 22903.
Telephone: (804) 977-4006
www.howellpress.com

Fifth Printing 2000

HOWELL PRESS

TABLE OF CONTENTS

INTRODUCTION

RED HOT LOVERS is a sizzling selection of hot and spicy American and international fare. It's written for daring and adventurous gourmets who appreciate the unconventional . . . for experimental Epicures who avoid the status quo and approach life with a "try anything once" attitude!

But, don't worry if your palate isn't lined with asbestos. We've developed each recipe to enable you to adjust the temperature! Simply identify the hot ingredients and season to taste. So, if you're reaching the point of "saying no" to bland sauces and find you are craving a little spiciness in your side dishes, then you're probably ready to become a RED HOT LOVER!

Caution: We do advise you, however, to familiarize yourself with all the "Vices and Spices" before you tempt your lover with a "Sultry Starter!" And, be sure you read each chapter and understand the importance of "Warming Up" before you prepare an entrée like "Smoldering Passions!"

Whether you're a culinary thrill-seeker or just need something to spice up your life, we're sure you'll find that RED HOT LOVERS has the perfect menu for any occasion. And, we guarantee you'll have a hot time tonight!

WARMING UP
(Presentation)

*H*ave you ever fantasized about a sultry evening in the tropics, dining on a veranda by moonlight, only yards from the ocean? You can almost feel the balmy breeze and hear the gentle surf! Now, let your mind wander to the romantic balcony setting of an intimate New Orleans café. Can you hear the street musicians yet? Or, let your daydream carry you to the tranquil setting of an oriental garden, your meal served quietly and expertly by exotic geishas! Now let your imagination jet you to the carefree and romantic atmosphere of a cozy sidewalk cantina overlooking the beach in Puerto Vallarta. Olé!

Throughout the world, wherever you find hot and spicy foods, you'll also find unique environments that are wonderfully conducive to romance. That's why we encourage you to make the most of your red hot dining experiences by creating an ambiance that complements the place of origin, or the title, of your entrée. Your efforts can be as simple and subtle as your selection of dinner music; some hot jazz would be perfect with an entrée like "I Wanna Be Loved Bayou!" Or, you can make a more complete statement by coordinating everything from the table setting to room accessories with your meal. Not only is it fun to create an exotic atmosphere, but it definitely gets the message across to your dining companion: this will be no ordinary evening! Here are some ideas.

An entrée like "It's Salsa Sudden" (orange roughy with papaya salsa) lends itself to a southwestern theme. You might begin by decorating the walls with a colorful sarape and arranging large earth-tone candles on the sideboard. Dress the table with heavily textured cream placemats over a turquoise table runner accented with red napkins in "silver" rings. A centerpiece composed of wild flowers and dried chili peppers will clearly signal to your lover that tonight will be hot!

"A Tropical Affair" definitely suggests the romance of the Caribbean. Begin with an aquamarine tablecloth and soft coral placemats. A centerpiece of seashells surrounding flickering candles will set the proper mood. Dine outside if the weather's warm and be sure to dress (or undress!) in tropical attire.

No matter how you play out any of our menus, the important thing is to play them up. Whatever hot scenario you have in mind for the evening can be realized easily with just a little imagination. Take it slow with an entrée like "Anticipation," and remember that getting there is half the fun! Or, go south of the border and act out your culinary fantasies with our recipe for a "Torrid Tango!" You can spice up your life with any of our tempting menus and become a red hot lover tonight!

VICES AND SPICES
(The Well-Stocked Pantry)

*D*on't miss out on a hot time tonight. Be sure you have all the spices to support your vices.

♥ ♥ ♥ ♥ ♥ ♥ ♥ ♥ ♥ ♥ ♥ ♥ ♥ ♥ ♥ ♥

Herbs and Spices:
Allspice
Basil
Bay leaves
Beau Monde (Spice Islands blend)
Caraway seeds
Cardamom
Cayenne pepper
Celery salt
Chervil
Chives, fresh
Cilantro, fresh
Cinnamon, whole stick
Cinnamon, ground
Cloves, ground
Coriander
Cumin
Curry
Dill, dried
Dill, fresh
Fennel
Garlic, powdered
Mace
Marjoram
Mustard, dry
Mustard seeds
Nutmeg
Oregano
Parmesan cheese
Turmeric

Spirits:
Brandy
Sherry, dry
Wine, burgundy
Wine, dry white

Produce (partial list):
Almonds
Apricots, dried
Arugula
Asparagus
Avocados
Bean sprouts
Broccoli
Carrots
Cashews
Celery
Chard
Chives
Cucumber
Endive
Garlic, whole clove
Ginger root
Green beans
Jicama
Leeks
Lemons
Lettuce, radicchio
Lettuce, romaine
Limes
Mushrooms
Onions, green
Onions, red
Onions
Papaya
Peanuts
Pecans
Peppers, Anaheim
Peppers, green
Peppers, jalapeño
Peppers, poblano
Peppers, red

Peppers, yellow
Pimentos
Pineapple
Pistachios
Radishes
Raisins, black
Raisins, golden
Snow peas
Spinach, fresh
Spinach, frozen
Tangerines
Tomatoes
Walnuts

Condiments and Staples:
Anchovy fillets
Anchovy paste
Artichoke hearts, canned
Bacon
Beans, black canned
Beans, black dried
Beans, garbanzo
Beans, kidney
Black-eyed peas, canned
Bread crumbs
Bread crumbs, Japanese*
Butter
Catsup
Chutneys, assorted
Clam juice
Coconut, shredded
Corn on the cob, baby canned
Cornstarch
Crackers, saltine
Cream, whipping
Hoisin sauce*
Honey

Horseradish
Mustard, Creole
Mustard, Dijon
Oil, chili
Oil, light olive
Oil, olive
Oil, peanut
Olives, black
Oranges, canned mandarin
Oyster sauce*
Peanut butter
Peppers, chile, canned diced
Peppers, chile, canned whole
Peppers, chipotle,
  canned in adobo sauce
Pine nuts
Smoke, liquid hickory
Soy sauce
Sour cream
Stock, beef
Stock, chicken
Sugar, brown
Tabasco sauce (hot pepper sauce)
Tomato juice
Tomato paste
Tomato sauce
Tomatoes, sundried in oil
Vinegar, cider
Vinegar, red wine
Vinegar, rice wine
Vinegar, tarragon
Vinegar, white wine
Water chestnuts, canned whole
Worcestershire sauce

*Available in oriental markets

♥ ♥ ♥ ♥ ♥ ♥ ♥ ♥ ♥ ♥ ♥ ♥ ♥ ♥ ♥ ♥ ♥

Ceviche

4 hours 15 minutes

Step One:

1/3 lb. ocean scallops,
  cut into bite-size pieces
1/4 lb. orange roughy
  (or other firm white fish),
  cut into bite-size pieces
5 limes, juiced

Combine scallops, fish, and lime juice in bowl and marinate 3 hours. Drain, rinse, and return to bowl.

Step Two:

2 Tbsp. olive oil
2 Tbsp. chopped red onion
2 Tbsp. minced parsley
2 tsp. minced cilantro
1 jalapeño pepper, seeded and
  minced
1 Tbsp. chopped pimento
1 clove garlic, minced
1/4 tsp. marjoram
salt to taste
2-6 drops Tabasco sauce
red leaf or butter lettuce

In a small bowl, combine all ingredients, except lettuce leaves. Pour over scallops and fish, mix gently, and marinate 1 hour at room temperature. Place lettuce leaves onto small plates. Drain ceviche, spoon onto lettuce leaves and serve. Note: The citric acid of lime juice cooks the fish as readily as heat would.

Mustard Shrimp

24 hours 20 minutes

Step One:
1 bay leaf
1 tsp. celery salt
1/2 tsp. cayenne pepper
12 medium shrimp

Fill saucepan with water until half full. Add seasonings and bring to a boil. Add shrimp and cook 2-5 minutes or until shrimp turn pink. Drain and plunge into cold water. Drain and peel shrimp.

Step Two:
3 Tbsp. oil
1/4 cup catsup
1 1/2 Tbsp. lemon juice
1 Tbsp. tarragon vinegar
2 Tbsp. Worcestershire sauce
1 Tbsp. horseradish or Creole
   mustard
1/4 cup chopped red onion

Combine all ingredients, blending well. Add shrimp, cover, and marinate in refrigerator overnight. Pour mixture into serving bowl. Place serving bowl on tray, surround bowl with parsley and lemon wedges. Provide toothpicks and serve with crackers or sourdough bread rounds.

Curried Meatballs

20 minutes

Step One:
cashews, coarsely chopped
pineapple, coarsely chopped
coconut, shredded
assorted chutneys

Prepare condiments, place in serving bowls, and set aside.

Step Two:
1/2 lb. lean ground beef
1 Tbsp. peanut oil
1/2 cup minced onion
1 tsp. curry powder
1/4 tsp. salt
1/8 tsp. cayenne pepper
1/2 cup beef broth
2 tsp. cornstarch
2 tsp. lemon juice

Roll ground beef into 1" balls. Place wok over high heat. Add oil and swirl to coat wok. Add beef balls in batches and brown on all sides. Remove to bowl, set aside. Add onion, stir-fry 1 minute. Add curry, salt, and cayenne, stir-fry 30 seconds. In a small bowl, blend cornstarch with broth, stirring until smooth. Add cornstarch mixture to wok, and bring to a boil, stirring until thickened. Stir in lemon juice and meatballs, heat through. Place large red lettuce leaf on small plate, spoon meatballs onto lettuce leaf and serve with condiments.

Lonestar Caviar

Step One:

1 can black-eyed peas
3/4 cup minced green pepper
1/2 cup minced onion
3 green onions, sliced
1 jalapeño pepper, seeded and minced

Combine all ingredients in mixing bowl.

Step Two:

1 clove garlic, minced
1/3 cup olive oil
2 Tbsp. lemon juice
1 tsp. Worcestershire sauce
1/4 tsp. dry mustard
1 anchovy fillet, mashed
salt to taste
1/2 tsp. marjoram
1/2 tsp. coriander
10 drops Tabasco sauce, or to taste

Blend all ingredients well. Add vegetable mixture, toss well. Refrigerate 1 hour. Serve with lime wedges and tortilla chips (homemade, if possible) or crackers.

Jalapeño Cheese Dip

8 oz. cream cheese, room temperature
4 oz. cheddar cheese, grated
1 jalapeño pepper, seeded and minced
1/2 tsp. Worcestershire sauce
4 drops Tabasco sauce or to taste
2 Tbsp. milk
1 pkg. frozen chopped spinach,
    cooked and squeezed dry
garlic powder to taste

In food processor, or with hand mixer, blend all ingredients together until smooth. (Thin with more milk if necessary.) Cover and refrigerate 30 minutes or until ready to serve. Serve with tortilla chips, crackers, or vegetable sticks.

Shrimp Balls

Step One:

8 oz. cheddar cheese, grated
6 oz. raw shrimp, cleaned,
  deveined, and finely chopped
1 Tbsp. canned diced chile
  peppers
1/2 tsp. seeded and minced
  jalapeño peppers

Combine all ingredients and mix well. Form into bite-size balls. (At this point, you may cover and refrigerate until ready to use.)

Step Two:

1 cup flour
1/2 cup cornstarch
3/4 tsp. baking powder
salt to taste
1 cup water, divided
2 Tbsp. vegetable oil
Japanese bread crumbs*

Mix flour, cornstarch, baking powder, and salt. Mix 1/2 cup of the water with the oil and add to dry ingredients, whisking until blended. Continue to add water until batter is consistency of pancake batter. Dip shrimp balls into batter (allowing excess to drip off), then roll in bread crumbs.

Step Three:

peanut oil
fresh parsley sprigs

Heat oil in frying pan until almost smoking. Fry several balls at a time until golden brown. Drain on paper towels. Arrange on serving tray and garnish with parsley sprigs.

*Available in oriental markets

Hot Crab Fondue

45 minutes

2 8-oz. pkgs. cream cheese
1/2 cup mayonnaise
1/4 cup sherry
8 oz. crabmeat
1 clove garlic, minced
1 tsp. prepared mustard
French bread, cubed

Preheat oven to 300°F. Thoroughly blend all ingredients, except French bread, and pour into baking dish. Bake for 45 minutes. Pour into fondue pot or chafing dish and adjust flame to low. Arrange bread in basket and serve.

Hot Cheese Balls

Step One:

2 cups grated Gruyère cheese
10 pecan halves, finely chopped
1 1/2 Tbsp. flour
1/2 tsp. paprika

Combine ingredients in bowl and set aside.

Step Two:

2 egg whites
1/2 tsp. cream of tartar
1/4 tsp. Tabasco sauce
1 Tbsp. dry sherry
1 jalapeño pepper, seeded and
    minced (or 2 Tbsp. canned diced
    chile peppers)

Beat egg whites and cream of tartar until very stiff. Fold in remaining ingredients. Fold egg mixture into cheese mixture.

Step Three:

corn oil
1 cup crushed saltine crackers
parsley sprigs

Pour oil into large saucepan to a depth of 2 inches. Heat over medium-high heat until just beginning to smoke. Form cheese mixture into bite-size balls, roll in cracker crumbs and fry until golden. Remove to paper towels. Arrange cheese balls on warm plate, garnish with parsley, serve immediately.

SULTRY STARTERS
(Soups and Salads)

Gazpacho

1 hour 40 minutes

Step One:

1 onion, finely chopped

1 cucumber, peeled and finely
  chopped

1 green pepper, seeded and finely
  chopped

6 medium tomatoes, blanched,
  peeled, and chopped

5 cloves garlic, minced

1/2 cup tomato juice

1/4 cup red wine vinegar

1/3 cup light olive oil

5-10 drops Tabasco sauce

2 Tbsp. minced chives

salt to taste

Put one half of each of the onion, cucumber, green pepper, and tomatoes into a bowl and set aside. Put remaining vegetables and ingredients into blender or food processor and purée. Add purée to vegetables in bowl. Thin, if necessary, with tomato juice. Cover and chill 1 hour or more. (The longer it chills, the better the flavors blend.)

Step Two:

4 slices homemade-style white
  bread, crusts removed

butter

garlic powder

Preheat oven to 400° F. Butter both sides of bread. Sprinkle with garlic powder. Trim to 1/2" cubes. Spread on baking sheet. Bake until golden, 10-15 minutes. Taste soup for seasoning just before serving, adding salt or Tabasco sauce, if necessary. Serve in chilled bowls and garnish with homemade garlic croutons.

Black Bean Soup

Step One:

1 lb. black beans

Rinse and soak beans overnight in 4 quarts cold water or bring to a boil for 2 minutes, turn heat off and let soak 1 to 2 hours. Drain.

Step Two:

2 Tbsp. oil
2 jalapeño peppers, seeded and minced
1 red onion, coarsely chopped
3 cloves garlic, chopped
2 ribs celery, chopped
1 carrot, chopped
2 bay leaves
1 Tbsp. cumin
1 tsp. chili powder
6 cups chicken broth
cilantro sprigs
4 thin strips pimento

Heat oil in large stockpot. Sauté jalapeños, onion, and garlic until tender. Add remaining ingredients and reserved beans. Bring to a boil, cover, simmer 2 hours or until beans are tender. Using food processor or blender, pureé half of soup and return to stockpot. Thin with water, if necessary. Garnish with cilantro sprigs and pimento.

Chipotle Cheddar Soup

Step One:

2 Tbsp. butter
1 large onion, minced
1 stalk celery, minced
1-2 chipotle chiles from prepared
    chiles in adobo sauce
1/2 tsp. chili powder
1/2 tsp. cumin
1 Tbsp. flour

Sauté onion and celery gently in butter until transparent, about 6 minutes. In a blender, purée chipotle chiles with the adobo sauce that clings to them as you remove them from the can. Add puréed chiles, chili powder, and cumin to the onion mixture. Sprinkle with flour and cook for 2 minutes.

Step Two:

3 cups chicken broth
2 cups half and half
2 cups grated sharp cheddar cheese
salt and pepper
1 Tbsp. minced parsley

Slowly add broth to the onion mixture, bring to a boil and simmer for 10 minutes. Stir in half and half. Add the cheese, stirring until the cheese is melted. Season to taste. Sprinkle with parsley.

Tease Me Greens

Step One:

4-5 slices sourdough bread, crusts
  removed
butter
1/4 tsp. garlic powder
1/4 tsp. Beau Monde seasoning

Preheat oven to 400°F. Butter both sides of bread and sprinkle with seasonings. Cut into 1/2" cubes and spread in one layer on baking sheet. Bake for 10-15 minutes or until golden.

Step Two:

3/4 lb. mixture of romaine,
  radicchio, endive, and arugula
3/4 cup coarsely grated Gruyère
  cheese
5-6 fresh mushrooms, sliced
1 avocado, cubed
1 pear, skinned and cut into
  bite-size chunks
1/4 cup pine nuts, toasted

Place greens, cheese, and mushrooms in salad bowl and toss gently. Evenly distribute avocado, croutons, pear, and pine nuts over greens and serve with Garlic Dressing (see below).

Garlic Dressing

6 Tbsp. olive oil
3 Tbsp. heavy cream
2 Tbsp. milk
2 Tbsp. lemon juice
2 cloves garlic
1 egg
1/2 tsp. dry mustard
1/2 tsp. salt
freshly ground pepper to taste
1 Tbsp. chopped parsley

Place all ingredients in blender. Blend for 2 minutes, cover and refrigerate until ready to use.

Fire and Ice Salad

(Tomato, Green Bean, Jicama, and Cucumber Salad
in Mustard Seed Vinaigrette)

Step One:

1/3 lb. green beans, cut in 1" pieces
8 Roma tomatoes, sliced
1 jicama, peeled and diced
1 cucumber, peeled and sliced
10 radishes, sliced
6 green onions, sliced

Steam beans until crisp-tender. Drain under cold running water until completely cooled. Drain until dry. In serving dish, arrange tomatoes, cucumbers, jicama, and green beans in rows. Sprinkle radishes over jicama and cucumbers, and green onions over all.

Step Two:

3/4 cup apple cider vinegar
1/4 cup water
4 1/2 tsp. sugar
1 1/2 tsp. celery salt
1 1/2 tsp. mustard seeds
1/8 tsp. freshly ground black pepper
1/8 tsp. cayenne pepper

Combine all ingredients in small saucepan and bring to a boil. Boil 1 minute, remove from heat and cool completely. Pour marinade over vegetables and chill 1 hour before serving.

Caliente Cravings Salad

1 hour 30 minutes

(Corn, Avocado, and Black Bean Salad
with Chili Vinaigrette)

Step One:

1 tsp. olive oil
1 jalapeño pepper, seeded and
  finely chopped

Heat oil in small frying pan. Add jalapeño and
sauté until slightly softened. Set aside.

Step Two:

1/3 cup cider vinegar
1/2 tsp. Dijon mustard
1/2 tsp. Worcestershire sauce
2/3 cup light olive oil
freshly ground black pepper

Combine vinegar, mustard, and Worcestershire
in bowl. Whisk oil into bowl in a slow, thin
stream until well blended. Add jalapeño
pepper and pepper to taste.

Step Three:

2 ears corn, steamed
1 can black beans, drained and rinsed
1 avocado, peeled, seeded, and cubed
8 Roma tomatoes, chopped
1/4 cup chopped green onion
1/3 cup chopped cilantro
1/2 cucumber, peeled and cubed
cilantro sprigs (optional)

Cut kernels from corn, put into large bowl.
Add remaining ingredients. Fold vinaigrette
from Step Two into vegetable mixture. Let
stand one hour, stirring occasionally. Mound
salad on chilled plates, garnish with sprigs of
fresh cilantro, if desired.

Casablanca Nights

2 hours 20 minutes

(Beef Nuggets with Tangerine and Raisins in Spicy Tomato Sauce)

Here's cooking with you, kid. Let's "play it again" after dinner!

Step One:

2 Tbsp. olive oil
1 lb. lean stew meat, cut into
  bite-size cubes
1 onion, chopped
1 jalapeño pepper, seeded and
  minced
1/4 cup chopped parsley
1 tsp. minced fresh ginger
1 stick whole cinnamon
1/2 tsp. cumin
1/4 tsp. turmeric
2 tomatoes, chopped
3 Tbsp. tomato paste
1/4 cup tomato juice
1/4 cup Burgundy wine
juice of 1 tangerine
4-8 drops Tabasco sauce

In large frying pan, heat oil over medium heat. Add meat, brown on all sides. Remove meat to a bowl, set aside. Add onions and jalapeño pepper to pan, sauté until soft. Add herbs and spices, sauté 30 seconds. Stir in remaining ingredients, return beef to pan. Cover and simmer over low heat 1 1/2 hours. Remove cinnamon stick.

Step Two:

1 cup rice

Cook rice according to package directions.

Step Three:

1/4 cup raisins
1/4 cup golden raisins
1 tangerine, divided into segments
nuts (peanuts, cashews, pistachios,
  etc.), chopped

Add raisins to pan, cover and simmer 25 minutes. Add tangerine segments. Simmer 5 minutes. Mound rice in center of plate. Spoon beef mixture over rice, sprinkle with chopped nuts, and serve.

SUGGESTED MENU

Temperatures Rising

Curried Meatballs

Sultry Starters

Tease Me Greens

Haute Cuisine

♥ *Casablanca Nights*

The Heat Is On!

Spiced Squash

Wine

Pinot Noir

A Red Hot Number

1 hour 45 minutes

(Hot and Spicy African Beef Stew)

That's you all right, but I'm calling the tunes tonight!

Step One:

2 Tbsp. oil
1 lb. lean stew beef, cut into
    bite-size cubes
1 red onion, chopped
2 large tomatoes, chopped
1 1/4 cups beef stock
1/2 tsp. ground cinnamon
1/4 tsp. cayenne pepper
salt and pepper
3 carrots, cut into 1" cubes
1 cup canned garbanzo beans
1 cup canned kidney beans

In large pot over medium heat, heat oil and brown beef on all sides. Drain excess oil. Add next five ingredients, salt and pepper to taste, and bring to a boil. Reduce heat and cover. Simmer 45 minutes. Add carrots, continue simmering 30 minutes longer. Add garbanzo and kidney beans during last 5 minutes of cooking time.

Step Two:

1 cup rice
1/2 tsp. turmeric
2 Tbsp. butter, melted
1/2 cup raisins
peanuts, chopped
1 Tbsp. chopped parsley

Cook rice according to package directions, stirring in turmeric at the same time you stir in rice. When rice is done, toss with butter and raisins, mound in individual au gratin dishes, spoon beef mixture in center and garnish with chopped peanuts and parsley.

Temperatures Rising

Jalapeño Cheese Dip

Sultry Starters

Caliente Cravings Salad

Haute Cuisine

A Red Hot Number

The Heat Is On!

Artichoke and New Potato Medley

Wine

Zinfandel

Romancin' the Rib

3 hours

(Short Ribs in Tangy Hot Barbecue Sauce)

I can't rib without you. Let's mess around!

Step One:

1 lb. boneless beef short ribs

Preheat broiler. Lay ribs in baking pan and broil 10 minutes, turning ribs often.

Step Two:

1 Tbsp. oil

1 large onion, chopped

2 cloves garlic, minced

2 large tomatoes, chopped

1 cup beef stock

3 Tbsp. cider vinegar

2 Tbsp. brown sugar

1 Tbsp. plus 1 tsp. Worcestershire sauce

1 Tbsp. Dijon mustard

1 tsp. cayenne pepper

1/4 tsp. paprika

1/4 tsp. turmeric

2 thick slices of lemon

10 parsley sprigs

Preheat oven to 350°F. Put oil in large ovenproof pot over medium heat and sauté onion and garlic until soft. Add remaining ingredients and blend thoroughly. Add ribs and their juices. Bring mixture to a boil. Turn heat off, cover ribs and put pan in oven to bake for 2 hours.

Step Three:

2 red potatoes, peeled and cut into bite-size pieces

3 carrots, peeled and cut into bite-size pieces

Add potatoes and carrots to ribs, continue baking 30 minutes longer, or until tender. Remove lemon and parsley. Skim sauce with a spoon to remove fat. Ladle ribs and vegetables onto warmed plates and serve.

SUGGESTED MENU

Temperatures Rising

Lonestar Caviar

Sultry Starters

Chipotle Cheddar Soup

Haute Cuisine

Romancin' the Rib

The Heat Is On!

Corn Cakes with Smoky Chipotle

Chile Sauce

Wine

Pinot Noir

♥ In-sin-diary Salad

(Orzo, Feta, and Sundried Tomato Salad)

... will give you hot lips, ready to spark up the evening!

Step One:

1 lb. orzo

Cook orzo in boiling salted water until al dente. Rinse immediately in cold water. Drain well. Spoon into 3-quart serving bowl.

Step Two:

3 tsp. light olive oil
1 tsp. cider vinegar
pinch cayenne pepper
salt
1/2 cup sundried tomatoes in olive oil
1/2 cup basil leaves, loosely packed
freshly ground pepper
4 oz. feta cheese, crumbled

Combine oil, vinegar, cayenne, and salt to taste in medium bowl. Slice tomatoes into matchsticks. Slice basil into 1/8"-wide ribbons. Add to bowl. Stir mixture into orzo. Season generously with pepper. Gently fold in feta. Chill.

Step Three:

3 Tbsp. light olive oil
1 Tbsp. cider vinegar
1/2 tsp. cayenne pepper
salt to taste
freshly ground pepper
1/2 lb. mixed greens such as butter
  and red leaf lettuces, radicchio,
  endive, and arugula

Whisk oil, vinegar, and seasonings together. Toss with greens. Arrange greens on chilled plates, top with orzo salad. Serve with crusty French bread.

SUGGESTED MENU

Temperatures Rising

Ceviche

Sultry Starters

Black Bean Soup

Haute Cuisine

♥*In-sin-diary Salad*

The Heat Is On!

Crusty French Bread

Wine

Sauvignon Blanc

♥ Sin-tillatin' Rhythms

2 hours 30 minutes

(Chilled Shrimp and Pasta Salad with Ginger-Lime Dressing)

... on a hot summer's night, can certainly whet the appetite.

Step One:

1/2 cup sliced green onions
1/2 cup rice wine vinegar
1/4 tsp. salt
2 Tbsp. honey
1 tsp. minced fresh ginger
4 Tbsp. fresh lime juice
1/8 tsp. chili oil
1/8 tsp. cayenne pepper
1/8 tsp. freshly ground pepper

Combine all ingredients in bowl and whisk until well blended.

Step Two:

1 lb. angel hair pasta

Cook pasta in boiling salted water until al dente. Rinse with cold water. Toss half of dressing with pasta in bowl. Cover and chill, stirring occasionally, 1 to 2 hours. Refrigerate remaining dressing.

Step Three:

1 tsp. vinegar
1 1/2 tsp. salt
2 cups snow peas, ends trimmed
   diagonally
1 lb. medium shrimp, shelled and
   deveined

Pour vinegar and salt into 2 quarts simmering water. Add snow peas. Cook until tender. Remove and rinse in cold water. Add shrimp to pan. Cook just until shrimp turn bright orange, drain and plunge immediately into cold water. Drain. Set shrimp and snow peas aside.

Step Four:

1 pear, peeled, cored, and sliced
   into thin bite-size pieces
1 avocado, cut into bite-size pieces
1/3 cup toasted almonds

Divide pasta between two chilled plates. Fold shrimp, snow peas, pears, and avocados into remaining dressing. Spoon mixture into center of pasta and sprinkle with toasted almonds.

SUGGESTED MENU

Temperatures Rising

Hot Cheese Balls

Sultry Starters

Gazpacho

Haute Cuisine

♥ *Sin-tillatin' Rhythms*

The Heat Is On!

Crusty French Bread

Wine

Gewürztraminer

♥ *The Forecast: Passion*

(Grilled Chicken Strips on a Bed of Greens with Raspberry Vinaigrette)

Let's start our own heat wave tonight!

Step One:

3 Tbsp. butter
2 cloves garlic, minced
1/2 jalapeño pepper, minced
1/2 tsp. minced ginger
1 Tbsp. grated orange peel
1/2 cup chopped cilantro
1/8 tsp. cayenne pepper
1 cup chicken stock
salt to taste

Sauté garlic, jalapeño, and ginger in butter until tender. Add remaining ingredients and simmer until mixture thickens and coats back of spoon.

Step Two:

1 cup orange juice
freshly ground pepper
1 Tbsp. butter
1 split chicken breast, skinned
  and boned

In small saucepan over medium heat, cook orange juice until reduced to syrup. Add stock mixture from Step One, season with pepper to taste. Whisk in butter. Place chicken in medium bowl. Pour half of orange sauce over chicken and stir to coat. Marinate while preparing vinaigrette.

Step Three:

1 Tbsp. raspberry vinegar
2 Tbsp. light olive oil
2 Tbsp. heavy cream
3 Tbsp. water
1/2 cup fresh raspberries
3/4 lb. mixed greens, such as
  arugula, radicchio, spinach,
  endive, chicory, butter lettuce,
  and red lettuce

Put all ingredients, except greens, into blender and whip until smooth. Toss vinaigrette with greens and arrange on dinner plates.

Step Four:

1/2 cup fresh raspberries

Remove chicken from marinade and grill over medium-high heat, brushing with additional orange sauce, until done. Slice breasts into thin strips and lay on top of salad greens. Garnish chicken and greens with fresh raspberries and serve.

Temperatures Rising

Hot Crab Fondue

Sultry Starters

Black Bean Soup

Haute Cuisine

♥ *The Forecast: Passion*

The Heat Is On!

Spiced Squash

Wine

Sauvignon Blanc

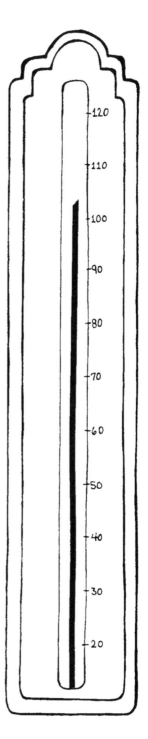

♥ In Hot Pursuit

(Grilled Chicken with Tomatillo Sauce)

You may live life in the fast lane, but I'll catch you tonight!

Step One:

3/4 cup fresh lime juice
2 Tbsp. olive oil
1/4 tsp. salt
1/4 tsp. pepper
2 chicken breasts, boned

Preheat grill or broiler. Combine lime juice, olive oil, salt, and pepper in shallow dish, blend thoroughly. Add chicken to marinade, turning to coat.

Step Two:

3 small tomatoes, chopped
6 green onions, sliced
1/2 jalapeño pepper, seeded and
   minced
2 Tbsp. chopped cilantro
2 Tbsp. olive oil
2 Tbsp. red wine vinegar
1 Tbsp. lime juice
1 clove garlic, minced
2-4 drops Tabasco sauce

Combine all ingredients in small bowl and blend thoroughly. Set salsa aside until ready to serve.

Step Three:

3 tomatillos, blanched and skinned
1/2 cup whipping cream
salt
lime wedges

Process tomatillos in blender or food processor until finely chopped. Pour into small saucepan over medium heat, add cream and simmer 5 minutes. Add salt to taste. Grill or broil chicken breasts 5 minutes per side, or until just done. Spoon tomatillo sauce into warmed au gratin dishes. Place chicken breasts on sauce and top with salsa. Garnish with lime wedges.

SUGGESTED MENU

Temperatures Rising

Jalapeño Cheese Dip

Sultry Starters

Tease Me Greens

Haute Cuisine

♥In Hot Pursuit

The Heat Is On!

Corn Cakes with Smoky Chipotle Chile Sauce

Wine

Sauvignon Blanc

♥ Smoldering Passions

(Chicken Stir-fry with Walnuts and Fresh Vegetables)

Where there's smoke there's fire. Let's fan the flames!

Step One:

3 Tbsp. soy sauce

2 Tbsp. cornstarch

2 Tbsp. dry sherry

1 tsp. minced ginger root

1 tsp. sugar

1/2 tsp. crushed red pepper

2-3 chicken breasts, skinned and
cut into 1" pieces

In small bowl, blend soy sauce into cornstarch. Add remaining ingredients and set aside.

Step Two:

1 cup rice

Cook rice according to package directions; keep warm.

Step Three:

2 Tbsp. peanut oil

1/2 green pepper, cut into
1" pieces

4 green onions, sliced diagonally
into 1" pieces

1 cup snow peas

1 cup walnut halves

1/2 cup whole water chestnuts

Heat wok (or large frying pan) over high heat. Add oil and swirl to coat sides of wok. Add peppers, onions, and snow peas, stir-fry 2 minutes or until crisp-tender. Remove and set aside. Add walnuts to wok and stir-fry 1-2 minutes. Remove and add to vegetables. Add more oil, if necessary. Drain chicken, reserving marinade. Add chicken to wok in batches and stir-fry 2 minutes. Stir in reserved marinade and cook until bubbly. Return vegetables and water chestnuts to wok, stir, cover, and cook 1 minute. Spoon over rice and serve immediately.

SUGGESTED MENU

Temperatures Rising

Shrimp Balls

Sultry Starters

Tease Me Greens

Haute Cuisine

♥ *Smoldering Passions*

The Heat Is On!

Asparagus Stir-fry

Wine

Chenin Blanc

A Tropical Affair

(Curried Chicken Breasts)

. . . is for those who dare. I double dare you tonight!

Step One:

1 Tbsp. peanut oil

1 medium onion, chopped

1 clove garlic, minced

1 tsp. minced ginger

1 tsp. curry powder

6 drops Tabasco sauce

2 chicken breasts, skinned and
  boned

1 large tomato, chopped

3/4 cup dry white wine

1 Tbsp. cider vinegar

2 tsp. brown sugar

1 tsp. chopped dill

1/2 cup raisins

1/2 cup golden raisins (optional)

In large frying pan, heat oil over medium heat. Add onion, garlic, and ginger. Sauté until onion is soft and translucent. Stir in curry powder and Tabasco sauce, cook 30 seconds. Add chicken and sauté 2-3 minutes per side. Stir in remaining ingredients, cover, and simmer 30 minutes.

Step Two:

1 Tbsp. chopped parsley

2 Tbsp. chopped cashews

Remove chicken to warmed au gratin dishes or dinner plates. Bring sauce to a boil and cook 5-8 minutes. Spoon over chicken, garnish with cashews and parsley, and serve.

SUGGESTED MENU

Temperatures Rising

Mustard Shrimp

Sultry Starters

Fire and Ice Salad

Haute Cuisine

A Tropical Affair

The Heat Is On!

Artichoke and New Potato Medley

Wine

Gewürztraminer

♥ Too Haute to Handle

(Chicken in Peanut Sauce with Julienne of Ham and Vegetables)

Is your body insured for meltdown?

Step One:

1 chicken breast, boned and
  skinned

Put chicken breast into simmering water and poach 10 minutes. Remove and cut into matchsticks.

Step Two:

3 Tbsp. peanut butter
1 1/2 tsp. soy sauce
1 Tbsp. red wine vinegar
2 Tbsp. peanut oil
1 1/2 tsp. crushed red pepper
1 1/2 tsp. minced ginger
1 large clove garlic, minced
1 Tbsp. dry sherry
1/4 tsp. cayenne pepper
1/2 tsp. white pepper

In small bowl, blend peanut butter, soy sauce, and vinegar until smooth. Add remaining ingredients and blend well.

Step Three:

20 snow peas

Trim snow peas and blanch by submerging briefly into boiling water until bright green. Drain and plunge into cold water. Drain and set aside.

Step Four:

1/4 lb. ham
1 bunch spinach leaves, washed
  and torn into bite-size pieces
1 cup bean sprouts
6-8 radishes, thinly sliced
2 tsp. sesame seeds

Cut ham into matchsticks. Toss the chicken and ham with the peanut butter mixture until thoroughly blended. Place a bed of spinach leaves on each dinner plate. Top with bean sprouts. Mound chicken mixture in center. Garnish with blanched snow peas, radishes, and sesame seeds and serve.

Temperatures Rising

Shrimp Balls

Sultry Starters

Tease Me Greens

Haute Cuisine

♥ *Too Haute to Handle*

The Heat Is On!

Asparagus Stir-fry

Wine

Riesling

♥ *Lover's Folly*

(Curried Chicken in Wine Sauce)

A good folly is worth whatever you pay for it. Go for broke and have a great one!

Step One:

1 lb. chicken pieces
1 tsp. seasoned salt
1/4 cup dry white wine
2 tsp. minced onion
1/2 tsp. curry powder
1/2 lb. mushrooms, sliced

Preheat oven to 350°F. Sprinkle seasoned salt over chicken. Place skin side down in baking dish. Mix remaining ingredients, pour over chicken. Cover and bake 30 minutes. Remove chicken to heated platter.

Step Two:

2 Tbsp. flour
1/4 cup water
2 Tbsp. snipped chives

Combine flour and water in small jar; shake to blend. Add to baking juices and whisk over medium heat until thickened. Pour sauce over chicken. Sprinkle with chives and serve.

SUGGESTED MENU

Temperatures Rising
Hot Cheese Balls

Sultry Starters
Tease Me Greens

Haute Cuisine
♥ Lover's Folly

The Heat Is On!
Garlic Herbed Potatoes

Wine
Sauvignon Blanc

Anticipation

(Chicken Breasts Simmered in Spices and Sour Cream)

Take it slow and remember, getting there is at least half the fun!

Step One:

3 Tbsp. butter
1 large red onion, sliced
2 cloves garlic, minced
1/2 tsp. cumin
1/2 tsp. minced ginger
1/4 tsp. turmeric
1/4 tsp. caraway seeds
1/8 tsp. cayenne pepper
2 large tomatoes, chopped
1/2 cup chicken stock
2 chicken breasts, skinned and
   boned

In large frying pan over medium heat, melt butter and sauté onions and garlic until soft. Add spices and cook 30 seconds. Stir in tomatoes and stock. Add chicken and bring to a boil. Reduce heat to low, simmer 10 minutes.

Step Two:

1 cup sour cream
1 tsp. brown sugar
1/8 tsp. cardamom
1/8 tsp. ground cloves
1/8 tsp. nutmeg
salt

Whisk ingredients together, salt to taste, cover and simmer 20 minutes. Uncover, simmer 20 minutes longer, stirring often.

Step Three:

1 cup rice
2 Tbsp. sliced green onions
3 Tbsp. chopped black olives

Cook rice according to package directions. Mound rice on warmed plates, arrange chicken breasts on top, and cover with sauce. Sprinkle with green onions and olives and serve immediately.

Temperatures Rising

Hot Cheese Balls

Sultry Starters

Caliente Cravings Salad

Haute Cuisine

Anticipation

The Heat Is On!

Sizzling Green Beans

Wine

Chenin Blanc

♥ Catfish on a Hot Tin Roof

1 hour 20 minutes

(Catfish Fillets with Spicy Herb-Tomato Sauce)

. . . will make you purr with a drawl!

Step One:

1 bay leaf
1/2 tsp. oregano
1/2 tsp. basil
1/4 tsp. each thyme, cayenne pepper,
   paprika, salt, white pepper, black
   pepper
2 Tbsp. butter
1/2 large tomato, chopped
1/2 cup chopped red onion
1/2 cup chopped green pepper
1 large clove garlic, minced

Combine all seasonings well and set aside. Melt butter in saucepan over medium heat. Add remaining ingredients, blend thoroughly, and sauté until vegetables soften.

Step Two:

1/2 cup clam juice
1/2 cup chicken stock
3/4 cup tomato sauce
1 Tbsp. tomato paste
2 Tbsp. red wine
2 tsp. sugar
1 tsp. Tabasco sauce
1/2 tsp. Worcestershire sauce

Add ingredients from Step Two to ingredients in Step One. Bring to a boil over high heat, then turn heat to low and simmer 25 minutes.

Step Three:

3 Tbsp. butter
2 Tbsp. flour
2 large catfish fillets

Preheat oven to 350°F. In small frying pan over medium heat, melt butter. Whisk in flour and cook until mixture is medium-brown in color (about 5 minutes). Whisk mixture into sauce and blend well. Cut two squares of foil large enough to enclose fillets. Place squares on cookie sheet, butter them and place a spoonful of sauce on each. Arrange fillets on sauce and top with more sauce. Fold foil to make packets and bake 30 minutes. Serve immediately.

SUGGESTED MENU

Temperatures Rising

Ceviche

Sultry Starters

Caliente Cravings Salad

Haute Cuisine

♥*Catfish on a Hot Tin Roof*

The Heat Is On!

Garlic Herbed Potatoes

Wine

Chenin Blanc

♥ Light My Fire

(Snapper Fillets in Chili-Lime Sauce)

I've got the kindling if you've got a match!

Step One:

1 Tbsp. olive oil

2 ribs celery, chopped

1 leek, chopped

1 cup clam juice

2 large tomatoes, chopped

1 4-oz. can jalapeño peppers,
  chopped

2 Tbsp. fresh lime juice

2 Tbsp. minced parsley

2 green onions, sliced

1 clove garlic, minced

2 Tbsp. dry white wine

4 drops Tabasco sauce

1/4 tsp. basil

Heat oil in large frying pan over medium heat. Add celery and leek, sauté until soft. Add remaining ingredients and bring to a boil. Reduce heat to low and simmer 15 minutes.

Step Two:

2 large snapper fillets

parsley sprigs

lime wedges

Add snapper fillets to sauce from Step One and simmer 20 minutes, or until done. Gently remove fish to warmed dinner plates and spoon sauce around fish. Garnish with sprigs of parsley and lime wedges.

SUGGESTED MENU

Temperatures Rising

Ceviche

Sultry Starters

Black Bean Soup

Haute Cuisine

♥*Light My Fire*

The Heat Is On!

*Corn Cakes with Smoky
Chipotle Chile Sauce*

Wine

Chenin Blanc

♥It's Salsa Sudden

(Orange Roughy Fillets with Fresh Papaya Salsa)

And it's also hot! We're playing with fire, let's not get caught!

Step One:

1 cup chopped papaya
2 tomatoes, chopped
2 green onions, minced
2 tsp. minced cilantro
1 Tbsp. olive oil
2 Tbsp. red wine vinegar
6-8 drops Tabasco sauce

Preheat oven to 350°F. Combine all ingredients in a small bowl and blend well. Refrigerate until ready to serve.

Step Two:

1/4 cup sugar
1/3 cup soy sauce
1 Tbsp. sherry
1 tsp. grated ginger
1 Tbsp. olive oil
1 Tbsp. sliced green onion
2 large orange roughy fillets

Combine all ingredients, except fish, in small bowl and blend well. Brush fillets with marinade and bake 15-20 minutes or until fish flakes easily when touched with a fork. Place fillets in warmed au gratin dishes and top with salsa. Serve immediately.

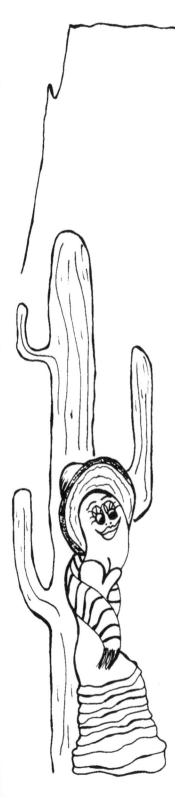

SUGGESTED MENU

Temperatures Rising

Lonestar Caviar

Sultry Starters

Chipotle Cheddar Soup

Haute Cuisine

♥*It's Salsa Sudden*

The Heat Is On!

Chili Chard Cups

Wine

Chenin Blanc

♥ I Wanna Be Loved Bayou

(Crayfish in Light Cream Sauce with Brandy and Spices)

. . . just you, no other body will do!

Step One:

2 Tbsp. butter

1/3 cup minced onion

Melt butter in small frying pan over medium heat. Add onion and sauté until soft.

Step Two:

3 Tbsp. butter

2 Tbsp. flour

1/4 cup whipping cream

2/3 cup milk

2 cups crayfish meat

1/2 tsp. salt

1/8 tsp. each white pepper, cayenne pepper, allspice, mace, and cloves

1 bay leaf

3 Tbsp. brandy

1 Tbsp. white wine

1 Tbsp. minced parsley

1/4 tsp. minced garlic

In large frying pan, melt butter over medium heat, whisk in flour and cook 10-15 minutes or until golden brown. Turn heat to low, and add onion mixture from Step One. Blend in cream, then milk, whisking constantly until thickened. Add crayfish. Blend well, add seasonings, brandy, and wine. Simmer 5 minutes. Stir in parsley and garlic. Simmer 10 minutes. Arrange a bed of lettuce leaves in individual au gratin dishes or on dinner plates. Spoon crayfish onto lettuce and serve immediately.

SUGGESTED MENU

Temperatures Rising

Hot Cheese Balls

Sultry Starters

Fire and Ice Salad

Haute Cuisine

♥I Wanna Be Loved Bayou

The Heat Is On!

Garlic Herbed Potatoes

Wine

Sauvignon Blanc

When You're Haute You're Haute

(Shrimp in Rich Cream Sauce with Bacon and Parmesan)   **40 minutes**

You ignite my passions.

Step One:

4 pieces bacon, diced
6 green onions, sliced
2 Tbsp. flour
1/4 cup milk
1/4 cup cream
3/4 cup sour cream
1/4 tsp. cayenne pepper or to taste
salt to taste
1 Tbsp. minced chives
1/2 tsp. marjoram
1/2 tsp. chervil
1 Tbsp. minced parsley
1/2 cup clam juice

Preheat oven to 400°F. In large frying pan over medium heat, sauté bacon and onions until bacon is crisp. Turn heat to low, whisk in flour. Whisk in milk, cream, and sour cream. Add seasonings, herbs, and clam juice. Simmer 5 minutes.

Step Two:

3/4 lb. medium shrimp, shelled
   and deveined
2 Tbsp. Parmesan cheese
1 Tbsp. minced parsley

Arrange shrimp in au gratin dishes, top with sauce, sprinkle with Parmesan. Bake 15 minutes. Sprinkle with parsley, serve immediately.

Temperatures Rising

Hot Crab Fondue

Sultry Starters

Tease Me Greens

Haute Cuisine

When You're Haute You're Haute

The Heat Is On!

Spinach Tomato Cups

Wine

Sauvignon Blanc

♥ Torrid Tango

(Shrimp and Crab Etouffée)

Just remember, it takes two!

Step One:

4 slices bacon, chopped
2 Tbsp. flour

In large frying pan over medium heat, brown bacon. Remove and set aside. Reduce heat to low, whisk flour into drippings and cook 20-30 minutes, or until mixture turns deep brown.

Step Two:

1 onion, chopped
2 ribs celery, chopped
1/2 green pepper, seeded and chopped
1/2 red pepper, seeded and chopped
2 tomatoes, chopped
3 Tbsp. tomato paste
1 large clove garlic, minced
1/2 tsp. marjoram
1 bay leaf
3/4 tsp. thyme
1/2 tsp. basil
1/2 tsp. freshly ground pepper
8-10 drops Tabasco sauce
1/4 tsp. cayenne pepper
1 tsp. Worcestershire sauce
2 cups cubed cooked ham
3/4 cup chicken broth
1/2 lb. shrimp, shelled and deveined
1/2 lb. crabmeat, cartilage removed

Add onion and celery to the mixture from Step One and cook until tender. Add all remaining ingredients (except crab and shrimp), bring to a boil. Turn heat to low, add crab and shrimp, simmer 1 hour.

Step Three:

1 cup rice
3 Tbsp. minced parsley

Cook rice according to package directions. Spoon seafood mixture over rice and sprinkle with parsley.

SUGGESTED MENU

Temperatures Rising

Shrimp Balls

Sultry Starters

Caliente Cravings Salad

Haute Cuisine

♥*Torrid Tango*

The Heat Is On!

Chard Chili Cups

Wine

Gewürztraminer

Hot Stuff

(Crab-stuffed Jalapeño Peppers with Guacamole)

Let me spice up your life!

Step One:

2 Tbsp. minced chives
2 Tbsp. minced green pepper
1 clove garlic, minced
1/4 cup grated Gruyère cheese
1 egg, beaten
1 1/2 cups flaked crabmeat
2 Tbsp. crushed saltine crackers
4 drops Tabasco sauce
1/8 tsp. dry mustard
1 can whole jalapeño peppers

Combine all ingredients, except jalapeño peppers, and blend well. Gently stuff peppers with crab mixture and place on dinner plate. Cover with wax paper and refrigerate 30 minutes or until ready to use.

Step Two:

1/2 avocado
1/2 tomato, chopped
2 Tbsp. minced chives
1 tsp. lemon juice
1/2 tsp. garlic salt
4 drops Tabasco sauce

Place avocado in medium-size bowl and mash. Add remaining ingredients and blend well. Refrigerate until ready to use.

Step Three:

2 Tbsp. peanut oil
1 cup crushed saltine crackers
2 eggs, beaten
sour cream

Heat oil in large frying pan over medium heat. Place cracker crumbs in one pie tin and eggs in another. Roll peppers in egg, then in crumbs. Repeat process until all peppers are coated. Fry stuffed peppers in oil until golden brown on all sides, drain on paper towels. Place peppers in warmed au gratin dishes, top with avocado mixture and a dollop of sour cream. Serve immediately.

SUGGESTED MENU

Temperatures Rising

Jalapeño Cheese Dip

Sultry Starters

Gazpacho

Haute Cuisine

♥ Hot Stuff

The Heat Is On!

Sizzling Green Beans

Wine

Sauvignon Blanc

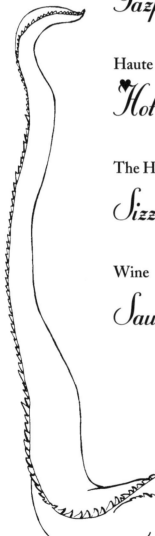

Bedeviled Bayou

(Crab and Shrimp Gumbo)

Bewitched by your spell. Beguiled, enchanted, for you I fell.

Step One:

5-7 fresh mustard leaves or small
   pkg. frozen mustard leaves,
   thawed
1/4 lb. fresh spinach leaves or
   small pkg. frozen spinach leaves,
   thawed
8 cups chicken broth
2 bay leaves
1 tsp. each thyme, oregano, savory,
   and basil
1/2 tsp. cayenne pepper
1/2 tsp. onion powder
1/2 tsp. garlic powder
1/4 tsp. each allspice, nutmeg,
   paprika, black pepper, and white
   pepper
1/8 tsp. ground cloves
1 cup rice

Tear or chop all greens into small pieces. Pour broth into large stockpot. Add herbs and spices. Bring to a boil. Turn heat to low, cover, and simmer while preparing Step Two. Cook rice according to package directions.

Step Two:

2 Tbsp. oil
1 large onion, chopped
1 green pepper, chopped
4 stalks celery (including tops),
   chopped
4 cloves garlic, chopped
1 lb. hot sausage (andouille,
   Italian, or kielbasa), sliced 1/4"
   thick
1 Tbsp. sugar
1 lb. medium shrimp, shelled and
   deveined
meat from 1 crab
3 Tbsp. minced parsley

Heat oil in large frying pan over medium heat. Add vegetables and garlic, cook until tender. Remove vegetables to stockpot. Add sausage, brown on both sides. Drain on paper towels, add to stockpot. Stir in sugar, cover and simmer 2 hours. Just before serving, add shrimp and crab, cooking until shrimp are bright orange. Place a large spoonful of rice into large soup bowls, ladle gumbo over rice. Sprinkle with parsley and serve with corn bread.

SUGGESTED MENU

Temperatures Rising

Mustard Shrimp

Sultry Starters

Tease Me Greens

Haute Cuisine

Bedeviled Bayou

The Heat Is On!

Corn Bread

Wine

Chenin Blanc

♥ Olive Me

(Lamb and Black Olives in Cumin Cream Sauce)

Why not take olive me?

Step One:

1 tsp. ground ginger
1 tsp. pepper
1/2 tsp. cumin
1/2 tsp. paprika
pinch saffron
2 cloves garlic, minced
1/2 tsp. salt
2 Tbsp. olive oil
1 lb. leg of lamb, cubed
3/4 cup minced leek
1/4 cup minced parsley
2 cups water

Put first eight ingredients into blender. Blend until consistency of paste. In a medium bowl, toss lamb with paste until coated. In large frying pan over low heat, sauté lamb 2-3 minutes. Add remaining ingredients, cover and simmer 2 hours.

Step Two:

1/2 cup black olives
1/2 tsp. lemon juice
salt and pepper
1/2 cup sour cream

Preheat oven to 200°F. Remove lamb to ovenproof dish, place in oven to keep warm. Using a soup spoon, skim off any excess oil from sauce. Increase heat to high and boil sauce until it thickens. Add olives and lemon juice, and season to taste. Fold in sour cream. Return lamb to sauce, heat through, but do not boil.

Step Three:

1 1/2 cups egg noodles

Cook noodles according to package directions. Drain and keep warm. Make a bed of hot noodles in warmed au gratin dishes, ladle lamb into center and serve.

Temperatures Rising

Curried Meatballs

Sultry Starters

Gazpacho

Haute Cuisine

♥Olive Me

The Heat Is On!

Sizzling Green Beans

Wine

Merlot

Some Like It Hot

1 hour 20 minutes

(Lamb Nuggets Tossed with Apricots, Raisins, and Spices)

Turn the flicker to a flame. Let's sizzle!

Step One:

1 lb. lamb shoulder, cubed
3 Tbsp. butter
1 large onion, chopped
1 tsp. coriander
1 tsp. cumin
1/2 tsp. cinnamon
1/2 tsp. minced ginger
1/8 tsp. saffron blended with
   1 Tbsp. hot red wine
1/8 tsp. cayenne pepper
freshly ground pepper
1-2 cups chicken stock

In large frying pan over medium heat, melt butter and brown lamb on all sides. Remove to bowl and set aside. Add onion, spices, and seasonings to pan; sauté until onion is soft. Return lamb to pan. Cover with stock. Reduce heat, cover and simmer 45 minutes.

Step Two:

1 cup dried apricots
1/2 cup raisins

Add apricots and raisins to pan. Simmer 20 minutes. Using a soup spoon, skim off any fat.

Step Three:

1 cup rice
nuts (pistachios, cashews,
   peanuts, etc.), chopped

Cook rice according to package directions. Mound rice in center of warmed dinner plates, spoon lamb over rice and garnish with chopped nuts. Serve immediately.

SUGGESTED MENU

Temperatures Rising

Curried Meatballs

Sultry Starters

Fire and Ice Salad

Haute Cuisine

♥*Some Like It Hot*

The Heat Is On!

Garlic Herbed Potatoes

Wine

Merlot

♥ Ewe Give Me Fever

1 hour 45 minutes

(Lamb with Jalapeños, Pineapple, and Pecans)

But I've got the cure!

Step One:

3 Tbsp. flour
1 lb. lamb shoulder, cut into
  bite-size pieces
3 Tbsp. butter
4 cloves garlic, chopped
2 onions, quartered
1/2 tsp. cumin
1/4 tsp. cayenne pepper
1/2 red pepper, seeded and cut into
  bite-size pieces
3 carrots, cut into bite-size pieces
1/2 cup chicken stock
1/4 cup dry white wine
salt

Put flour in plastic bag. Add lamb cubes and shake to coat. In large frying pan over medium heat, melt butter and brown lamb cubes in two batches. Add garlic and onion, sauté until soft. Remove lamb to bowl and set aside. Stir in cayenne pepper and cumin, cook 30 seconds. Add remaining ingredients, salt to taste, and bring to a boil. Reduce heat to low and simmer, covered, 15 minutes.

Step Two:

2 Tbsp. peanut oil
3/4 cup pecans
1 poblano chile pepper, seeded and
  minced
1/4 cup chicken stock

In small frying pan over medium heat, sauté pecans in oil 2-3 minutes. Remove pecans to a blender or food processor, reserve oil. Add pepper and broth to blender and purée. Return purée to oil and sauté over medium heat 3-4 minutes, whisking constantly.

Step Three:

1/2 fresh pineapple, peeled, cored,
  and cut into bite-size pieces
2 tomatoes, chopped
pinch cinnamon

Stir purée, half the pineapple, tomatoes, and cinnamon into lamb mixture. Continue cooking over low heat for 45 minutes. Add remaining pineapple and continue cooking 15 minutes longer.

Step Four:

1 cup rice
2 Tbsp. minced parsley

Cook rice according to package directions. Mound rice in warmed au gratin dishes. Spoon lamb over rice, sprinkle with parsley, and serve.

SUGGESTED MENU

Temperatures Rising

Lonestar Caviar

Sultry Starters

Fire and Ice Salad

Haute Cuisine

♥Ewe Give Me Fever

The Heat Is On!

Spinach Tomato Cups

Wine

Pinot Noir

♥In Love Again

(Gingered Pork Balls In Hot Orange Sauce)

It's sow easy to fall in love!

Step One:

1 orange

Remove peel of orange in long strips with vegetable peeler. Cut peel into matchsticks and blanch in boiling water 3 minutes. Drain and set aside.

Step Two:

3/4 lb. lean ground pork
1/3 cup chopped water chestnuts
1 egg
2 tsp. minced ginger
1 clove garlic, minced
1/4 tsp. pepper

Combine all ingredients thoroughly, roll into 1" balls and set aside.

Step Three:

3 Tbsp. peanut oil
8 green onions, sliced diagonally
    into 1" pieces
1/2 cup whole water chestnuts
1 jalapeño pepper, seeded and
    minced

In large frying pan, heat oil over medium-high heat. Add orange peel from Step One, green onions, water chestnuts, and jalapeño pepper. Sauté 1 minute. Remove to bowl and set aside. Add pork balls and brown on all sides until crusty (about 15 minutes). Drain oil. Return jalapeño mixture to pan, toss gently.

Step Four:

1/4 tsp. Tabasco sauce
1/4 cup Hoisin sauce*
3 Tbsp. peanut oil
2 Tbsp. soy sauce
1 can mandarin oranges, drained
chopped peanuts or sesame seeds

Combine Tabasco, Hoisin sauce, peanut oil, and soy sauce in small bowl and mix well. Add to pan and toss until pork is coated. Spoon pork into lettuce-lined au gratin dishes, garnish with mandarin oranges and chopped peanuts. Serve immediately.

*Available in oriental markets

Temperatures Rising

Mustard Shrimp

Sultry Starters

Tease Me Greens

Haute Cuisine

In Love Again

The Heat Is On!

Asparagus Stir-fry

Wine

Riesling

Hot Line

(Stir-fried Pork with Broccoli and Snow Peas)

For a good time, pick up the phone and call me!

Step One:

3/4 lb. boneless pork loin chops, trimmed
2 tsp. cornstarch
1/4 cup soy sauce
1/3 cup water
3/4 tsp. white pepper

Partially freeze pork (meat should not be hard, but firm with some ice crystals; this process usually takes 30-45 minutes). Slice into very thin (1/8" or less) 2"-long strips. Blend cornstarch, soy sauce, water, and pepper. Add pork to mixture and set aside.

Step Two:

1 cup rice

Cook rice according to package directions. Keep warm.

Step Three:

2 Tbsp. peanut oil
1 tsp. minced ginger
1 large clove garlic, minced
1/2 head broccoli, cut into florets
24 snow peas
3/4 cup whole water chestnuts

Place wok (or large frying pan) over medium-high heat. Add oil and swirl to coat wok. Add ginger and garlic, stir-fry 30 seconds. Add broccoli, stir-fry 3 minutes. Add snow peas and water chestnuts and stir-fry 2 minutes. Remove vegetables to bowl. Drain pork, reserving marinade. Add half of pork to wok and stir-fry 2-3 minutes. Remove to a bowl and repeat with remaining pork. Return all pork to wok. Add marinade and stir until bubbling. Return vegetables to wok, cover and cook 1 minute. Mound rice in center of warmed dinner plates. Top with pork and vegetables and serve immediately.

SUGGESTED MENU

Temperatures Rising

Shrimp Balls

Sultry Starters

Chipotle Cheddar Soup

Haute Cuisine

Hot Line

The Heat Is On!

Spinach Tomato Cups

Wine

Sauvignon Blanc

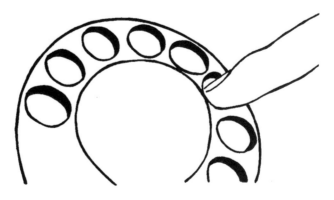

♥ Five-Alarm Love Affair

2 hours

(Stuffed Wontons in Hot Tomato Sauce)

Wanna have a fire drill?

Step One:

1 cup finely chopped onion
3 Tbsp. diced jalapeño chilis
1 Tbsp. butter
1 cup corn kernels
1 tsp. minced cilantro
1 tsp. cumin
1 tsp. oregano
pinch cayenne pepper

Sauté onion and jalapeño in butter over medium heat until tender. Add corn and herbs and continue cooking for 3-5 minutes. Remove to bowl and refrigerate for 1 hour.

Step Two:

2 Tbsp. olive oil
4 garlic cloves, minced
6 green onions, minced
2 tomatoes, diced
1/4 cup chopped basil
1 tsp. grated orange peel
1/2 tsp. each sugar, thyme,
    oregano, rosemary, and pepper
pinch crushed red pepper

Heat oil in frying pan over medium heat. Sauté garlic and onions until tender. Add remaining ingredients and simmer 15-20 minutes.

Step Three:

1 tsp. salt
1 tsp. oil

Fill a 6-quart stockpot halfway with water. Add salt and oil. Bring to a simmer.

Step Four:

1 1/2 cups grated Monterey Jack
    cheese
basil leaves (optional)
50 wonton wrappers

Blend cheese into corn and chili mixture. Moisten edges of the wonton wrappers with water, using a small kitchen brush. Mound a teaspoon of filling on each wrapper and fold the wrapper diagonally to form a triangle. Pinch edges and crimp with a pasta wheel. Repeat process until you have used up all the filling. Add wontons to simmering water in small batches and cook gently for 4 minutes. Drain wontons, spoon sauce over them and garnish with basil leaves, if desired.

FIRE ALARM
IN CASE OF FIRE BREAK GLASS

SUGGESTED MENU

Temperatures Rising

Shrimp Balls

Sultry Starters

Caliente Cravings Salad

Haute Cuisine

♥ *Five-Alarm Love Affair*

The Heat Is On!

Spinach Tomato Cups

Wine

Pinot Noir

ѕicy Hot Dare

(ѕausage and Noodle Pie)

. . . aaus adventurous flair. I cayenne, if you cayenne!

Step One:

8 oz. egg noodles

Preheat oven to 350°F. Cook noodles according to package directions until barely al dente. Drain and set aside.

Step Two:

1/3 lb. hot Italian sausage

Cook sausage in frying pan over medium heat, breaking meat into small pieces. Drain on paper towels, set aside.

Step Three:

2 Tbsp. butter

2 cloves garlic, minced

In small pan, sauté garlic in butter over medium heat until tender.

Step Four:

4 eggs

1/2 cup grated jalapeño jack cheese

1 tsp. paprika

1 tsp. minced rosemary

1/8 tsp. cayenne pepper

rosemary sprigs

cherry tomatoes, halved

Beat eggs in large bowl. Add remaining ingredients, the noodles from Step One, the garlic butter from Step Three and blend well. Fold in sausage. Pour into greased 10-inch quiche pan. Bake until golden, about 30-35 minutes. Cut into four wedges and garnish with sprigs of rosemary and halved cherry tomatoes.

SUGGESTED MENU

Temperatures Rising

Mustard Shrimp

Sultry Starters

Fire and Ice Salad

Haute Cuisine

A Spicy Hot Dare

The Heat Is On!

Chard Chili Cups

Wine

Chenin Blanc

.h Song

.h Creamy Tomato-Herb Sauce and Toasted Pine Nuts)

A ь̠ ng could spark an interest. Can you handle the heat?

Step One:

1 Tbsp. light olive oil

8 Roma tomatoes, peeled and finely chopped

4 cloves garlic, minced

1 green pepper, chopped

1 red onion, chopped

6 mushrooms, sliced

1/4 tsp. each marjoram, oregano, savory, rosemary, and thyme

1/8 tsp. fennel seeds, crushed

pinch crushed red pepper

Heat olive oil in frying pan over medium heat. Add all ingredients and sauté until tender.

Step Two:

1/2 cup hearty red wine

1/2 cup water

1/2 cup heavy cream

4 Tbsp. butter

salt

freshly ground pepper

1/2 cup toasted pine nuts

Add wine and water to sauce from Step One, simmer for 10 minutes. Pour sauce into blender or processor and purée. Return to pan, whisk in cream. Whisk in butter. Season with salt and pepper to taste. Stir in pine nuts. Keep warm. Do not boil.

Step Three:

24 cheese ravioli

1/4 cup grated fresh Parmesan cheese

Cook ravioli in gently boiling water until al dente. Drain and divide between two warm plates. Ladle sauce over ravioli and sprinkle with Parmesan.

Temperatures Rising

Hot Crab Fondue

Sultry Starters

Fire and Ice Salad

Haute Cuisine

A Torch Song

The Heat Is On!

Spinach Tomato Cups

Wine

Pinot Noir

♥ Try A Little Tinder-ness

(Wild Rice Cakes with Mélange of Peppers and Portobello Mushrooms)

You've got to do more than rub two sticks together when you want to set hearts afire.

Step One:
1/2 red pepper
1/2 yellow pepper
1/2 green pepper
1/2 Anaheim pepper

Roast peppers over gas flame or under the broiler until skin blisters. Put into paper bag and close tightly to steam peppers. Set aside.

Step Two:
4 oz. wild rice
1 Tbsp. salt

Bring 1 quart water to a boil. Add salt and rice. Cover, simmer 30 minutes. Drain in colander, rinse with cold water.

Step Three:
1 Tbsp. butter
1 Tbsp. vegetable oil
1/2 cup minced onion
1 small carrot, minced
5-6 mushrooms, coarsely chopped
1/4 cup flour
1 slice fresh bread, crumbled
1/2 tsp. thyme
1/8 tsp. cayenne pepper
salt and pepper to taste
2 medium eggs, beaten

Heat oil and butter in frying pan over medium heat, and sauté onion, carrot, and mushrooms until soft. Blend in flour, cook 1 minute. Stir in remaining ingredients, blend mixture into rice. Shape into 2"-wide round cakes. Set aside. Remove skin from steamed peppers from Step One. Slice peppers diagonally, making diamonds.

Step Four:
2 Portobello mushrooms, sliced
  1/4" thick
3 Tbsp. butter
1 large clove garlic, minced
1 Tbsp. balsamic vinegar
1/2 cup chicken stock
2 Tbsp. butter
fresh basil leaves

Sauté mushrooms, garlic, and peppers in butter until soft. Remove peppers and mushrooms. Add vinegar and stock to pan and boil until reduced to 1/4 cup. Whisk in butter. Return mushrooms and peppers to pan.

Step Five:
1 Tbsp. butter

In clean frying pan, melt butter over medium heat. Brown rice cakes on both sides. Pour sauce, peppers, and mushrooms over rice cakes.

Temperatures Rising

Jalapeño Cheese Dip

Sultry Starters

Caliente Cravings Salad

Haute Cuisine

♥*Try A Little Tinder-ness*

The Heat Is On!

Chard Chili Cups

Wine

Merlot

Spinach Tomato Cups

30 minutes

Step One:

2 slices bacon, chopped

Preheat oven to 350°F. In frying pan, brown bacon until crispy. Drain on paper towels.

Step Two:

1 large firm tomato
salt and pepper

Halve tomato, scoop out pulp and discard. Sprinkle tomato with salt and pepper to taste. Set aside.

Step Three:

3/4 cup water-packed artichoke hearts, drained
1/2 cup frozen chopped spinach, thawed and squeezed dry
1 green onion, sliced
1 oz. cream cheese, room temperature
1 Tbsp. sour cream
1 Tbsp. butter
1 tsp. basil
1/4 cup Parmesan cheese

Chop artichoke hearts. Put bacon, spinach, and artichoke hearts in food processor. Add remaining ingredients and process until well blended. Stuff mixture into tomato halves.

Step Four:

1 Tbsp. bread crumbs
1 Tbsp. melted butter
1 Tbsp. chopped slivered almonds

Combine all ingredients, mix well and spoon over tops of tomatoes. Place tomatoes in lightly greased baking dish and bake, uncovered, 10 minutes.

Sizzling Green Beans

40 minutes

Step One:

1/2 lb. green beans

Snap off ends of green beans and cut them into 3" lengths. Put green beans in large pot of boiling water. Boil 5-7 minutes, drain and plunge into ice water.

Step Two:

2 Tbsp. olive oil
1/2 tsp. crushed red pepper
1 clove garlic, minced
1 large tomato, chopped
2 Tbsp. chopped parsley
1 tsp. basil
1/2 tsp. thyme
1/2 tsp. oregano
salt and pepper
Parmesan cheese

Heat olive oil in large frying pan over medium heat. Add crushed red pepper and cook 1 minute. Remove pepper flakes. Add garlic, tomatoes, and seasonings. Turn heat to low and simmer, covered, 20 minutes. Add green beans. Heat through, about 8-10 minutes. Sprinkle with Parmesan cheese and serve.

Artichoke and New Potato Medley

30 minutes

Step One:

5 new potatoes

In small saucepan over high heat, boil new potatoes until just tender. Drain, peel, and slice into 1/8" slices.

Step Two:

1/2 cup sour cream
1 1/2 tsp. anchovy paste
1/4 tsp. white pepper
1/2 cup artichoke hearts, cut into
   bite-size pieces
10 black olives, chopped
1/8 tsp. garlic salt
5 drops Tabasco sauce
1/2 tsp. paprika
1 tsp. tarragon vinegar

Combine all ingredients with potatoes and simmer in saucepan over low heat for 10 minutes. Spoon medley into serving bowl and serve immediately.

Chard Chili Cups

Step One:

2 Tbsp. olive oil

1/2 bunch spinach, stems removed, chopped

1/2 bunch chard, stems removed, chopped

2 cloves garlic, minced

1 small onion, chopped

2 jalapeño peppers, seeded and minced

Heat oil in large frying pan over medium heat. Add remaining ingredients and sauté until just wilted, 5-7 minutes.

Step Two:

butter

4 eggs

1/2 cup sour cream

3/4 cup grated Monterey Jack cheese

5 drops Tabasco sauce

salt and pepper

paprika

Preheat oven to 350°F. Butter individual ramekins or a loaf pan. Combine ingredients, except seasonings, in large bowl. Add salt and pepper to taste. Add vegetable mixture and blend well. Pour into ramekins and sprinkle with paprika. Bake 25-30 minutes or until golden on top. Let stand 5 minutes before serving.

Spiced Squash

15 minutes

Step One:

2 cups cubed butternut squash

Steam squash until just tender.

Step Two:

2 Tbsp. butter

pinch mace

salt and pepper

2 Tbsp. toasted pine nuts

2 Tbsp. Parmesan cheese

Melt butter in frying pan over low heat, whisking frequently until golden brown. Add mace, salt and pepper to taste. Sauté 2 minutes. Add squash from Step One and pine nuts, heat through, toss with Parmesan and serve immediately.

Asparagus Stir-fry

Step One:

1/2 cup water
1 Tbsp. sliced ginger
1/2 tsp. freshly ground pepper
1/2 tsp. white pepper
1/2 tsp. crushed red pepper
1 tsp. salt

Combine all ingredients in a saucepan and bring to a boil. Lower heat and simmer 10 minutes.

Step Two:

2 Tbsp. peanut oil
1 clove garlic, sliced
3 stalks asparagus, sliced diagonally
24 snow peas, trimmed
2/3 cup whole water chestnuts
8-10 canned baby corn on the cob
    (optional)
1/4 red pepper, julienned
8-10 large mushrooms, sliced
4 green onions, sliced diagonally
2 cups bean sprouts
1 tsp. soy sauce

Heat wok (or large frying pan) over high heat. Add oil and swirl to coat sides of wok. Stir-fry garlic, asparagus, and snow peas for 2 minutes. Add 2 Tablespoons of liquid from Step One. Add remaining ingredients and stir-fry 1 minute. Spoon into warmed serving bowl and serve immediately.

Garlic Herbed Potatoes

40 minutes

Step One:

1/4 lb. small new potatoes, peeled

Steam or boil new potatoes until tender.

Step Two:

1 Tbsp. butter
2 cloves garlic, minced
2 Tbsp. lemon juice
2 Tbsp. minced parsley
1/2 tsp. each thyme, rosemary,
    paprika, and pepper
pinch cayenne pepper
salt

Melt butter in small frying pan over medium heat. Sauté garlic 2-3 minutes, add potatoes and remaining ingredients. Salt to taste. Sauté until heated through, serve immediately.

Corn Cakes with Smoky Chipotle Chile Sauce

Step One:

1 cup cornmeal
3/4 tsp. baking soda
3/4 tsp. salt
1/8 tsp. cayenne pepper

Stir ingredients together in mixing bowl.

Step Two:

2 eggs, beaten
1 cup whipping cream
1 cup corn kernels
1/2 cup grated cheddar cheese
1/4 cup chopped cilantro
3 Tbsp. canned diced chile peppers
2 tsp. grated orange peel

Whisk all ingredients together. Blend with dry ingredients from Step One until smooth. If necessary, add more cream to make batter the consistency of pancake batter. Set aside.

Step Three:

1 Tbsp. olive oil
1 large red pepper, minced
1 small pepper from prepared chipotle
  peppers in adobo sauce
1 tsp. Worcestershire sauce
1/8 tsp. liquid hickory smoke

In small frying pan over medium heat, sauté red pepper in oil until tender. Pour into blender, add remaining ingredients, and purée. Set aside.

Step Four:

1 Tbsp. butter
cilantro sprigs

Brush hot griddle with butter. Drop 1 Tablespoon of batter on griddle for each cake. Fry until golden brown on each side. Remove to warm plates. Garnish with sprigs of fresh cilantro and serve with chili sauce.

SUBJECT INDEX

Fish

RECIPE INDEX

COOLING DOWN
(Notes)

COOLING DOWN
(Notes)

COOLING DOWN
(Notes)

COOLING DOWN
(Notes)